My United States

Colorado

JENNIFER ZEIGER

Children's Press®
An Imprint of Scholastic Inc.

Content Consultant

James Wolfinger, PhD, Associate Dean and Professor
College of Education, DePaul University, Chicago, Illinois

Library of Congress Cataloging-in-Publication Data
Names: Zeiger, Jennifer, author.
Title: Colorado / by Jennifer Zeiger.
Description: New York : Children's Press, an imprint of Scholastic Inc., 2018. | Series: A true book | Includes bibliographical
    references and index.
Identifiers: LCCN 2017004662 | ISBN 9780531252536 (library binding) | ISBN 9780531232835 (pbk.)
Subjects: LCSH: Colorado—Juvenile literature.
Classification: LCC F776.3 .Z45 2018 | DDC 978.8—dc23
LC record available at https://lccn.loc.gov/2017004662

Photographs ©: cover: Kennan Harvey/Getty Images; back cover ribbon: AliceLiddelle/Getty Images; back cover: David Clifford/
Getty Images; 3 bottom: SFM GM WORLD/Alamy Images; 3 map: Jim McMahon; 4 right: Missing35mm/iStockphoto; 4 left:
dell640/iStockphoto; 5 top: Ron_Thomas/iStockphoto; 5 bottom: Minden Pictures/Superstock, Inc.; 7 center bottom: Dennis
MacDonald/age fotostock; 7 center top: Nadja Rider/Shutterstock; 7 bottom: Jaminnbenji/Shutterstock; 7 top: sumikopho-
to/Shutterstock; 8-9: Ron_Thomas/iStockphoto; 11: Maciej Bledowski/iStockphoto; 12: Natalie Jezzard/Alamy Images; 13:
THEPALMER/iStockphoto; 14: Ron_Thomas/iStockphoto; 15: RichardSeeley/iStockphoto; 16 inset: Trong Nguyen/Shutterstock;
16-17 main: Jeff Zehnder/Shutterstock; 19: Rick Wilking/REUTERS/Alamy Images; 20: Tigatelu/iStockphoto; 22 right: Brothers
Good/Shutterstock; 22 left: Atlaspix/Shutterstock; 23 center: Francois Gohier/Western Paleontological Labs/Science Source; 23
bottom left: RichardSeeley/iStockphoto; 23 top center: Minden Pictures/Superstock, Inc.; 23 bottom right: sbonk/iStockphoto;
23 top left: Missing35mm/iStockphoto; 23 top right: J-Palys/iStockphoto; 24-25: Peter V. Bianchi/Getty Images; 27: John K.
Hillers/The Granger Collection; 29: Science Source; 30 right: Science Source; 31 right: Everett Historical/Shutterstock; 31 left:
Atlaspix/Shutterstock; 32: Johnston, Frances Benjamin, 1864-1952/Library of Congress; 33: DEA PICTURE LIBRARY/Getty Images;
34-35: digitalfarmer/iStockphoto; 36: dell640/iStockphoto; 37: Lezlie Sterling/ZUMA Press/Newscom; 38: Cyrus McCrimmon/
Getty Images; 39: RJ Sangosti/Getty Images; 40 inset: Olga Nayashkova/Shutterstock; 40 bottom: PepitoPhotos/iStockpho-
to; 41: Created by MaryAnne Nelson/Getty Images; 42 top left: The Granger Collection; 42 top right: Library of Congress; 42
bottom left: Library of Congress; 42 bottom right: Roger Viollet/Getty Images; 43 top: The Granger Collection; 43 center right:
Everett Collection; 43 center left: ullstein bild - snapshot-photography/Tobias Seeliger/The Granger Collection; 43 bottom left:
Featureflash Photo Agency/Shutterstock; 43 bottom center: Everett Collection Inc/Alamy Images; 43 bottom right: BrunoRosa/
Shutterstock; 44 top: SNEHIT/Shutterstock; 44 bottom left: Claudio Del Luongo/Shutterstock; 44 bottom right: Peter Maerky/
Shutterstock; 45 top left: Atlaspix/Shutterstock; 45 top right: Jaminnbenji/Shutterstock; 45 center: sumikopho/Shutterstock;
45 bottom: Peter V. Bianchi/Getty Images.

Maps by Map Hero, Inc.

**Front cover: A man ice climbing
a frozen waterfall in Silverton**

Back cover: A kayaker in Carbondale

Welcome to Colorado

Find the Truth!

Everything you are about to read is true **except** for one of the sentences on this page.

Which one is **TRUE**?

T or F People have farmed in Colorado since about 2000 BCE.

T or F Colorado was one of the 13 original U.S. states.

Find the answers in this book.

UNITED STATES

← Colorado

Contents

THE BIG TRUTH!

Rocky Mountain
Columbine

What Represents Colorado?

A skier in Colorado

Quaking
aspen trees

Claret
Cup cactus

This Is Colorado!

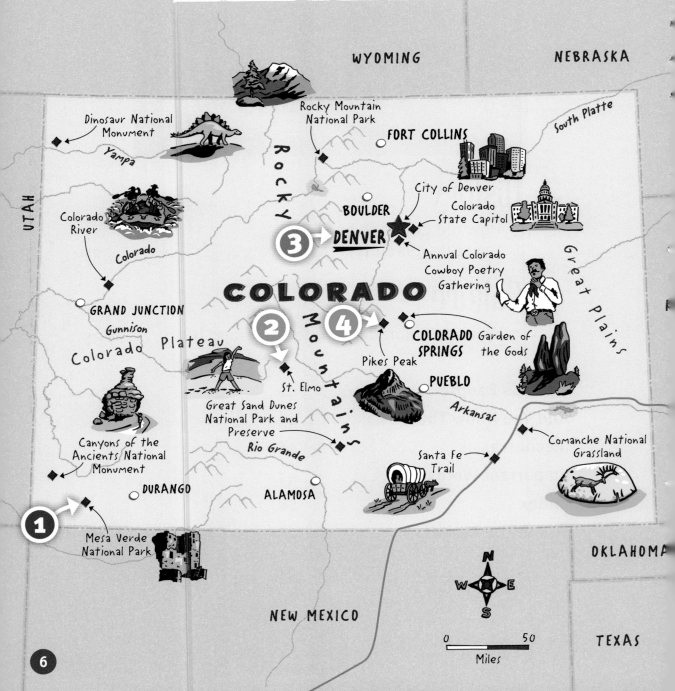

WYOMING

NEBRASKA

Dinosaur National Monument

Rocky Mountain National Park

Yampa

South Platte

FORT COLLINS

UTAH

Colorado River

Colorado

City of Denver

Colorado State Capitol

BOULDER

③ → DENVER

GRAND JUNCTION

Gunnison

Colorado Plateau

②

Annual Colorado Cowboy Poetry Gathering

COLORADO

④ →

Great Plains

St. Elmo

Mountains

Pikes Peak

COLORADO SPRINGS

Garden of the Gods

Great Sand Dunes National Park and Preserve

Rio Grande

PUEBLO

Arkansas

Canyons of the Ancients National Monument

Santa Fe Trail

Comanche National Grassland

① →

DURANGO

ALAMOSA

Mesa Verde National Park

NEW MEXICO

OKLAHOMA

N
W E
S

0   50
Miles

TEXAS

➊ Mesa Verde National Park

Boasting thousands of ancient sites, Mesa Verde National Park should not be missed. The Ancestral Pueblo people lived here for roughly 700 years before disappearing sometime about 1300 CE.

➋ Saint Elmo

Founded in 1880, Saint Elmo is one of Colorado's many old mining towns. When the gold ran out and the mine closed in 1922, nearly everyone in the town left. Today, tourists can visit the town's remaining buildings.

➌ U.S. Mint

Do you know how money is made? You can see for yourself at the U.S. Mint facility in Denver. One of just six U.S. Mint facilities in the country, it produces tens of millions of coins each day.

➍ Pikes Peak

Pikes Peak is the most visited mountain in the country. It is named after explorer Zebulon Pike, who discovered it in 1806. He tried to reach the summit but never made it to the top.

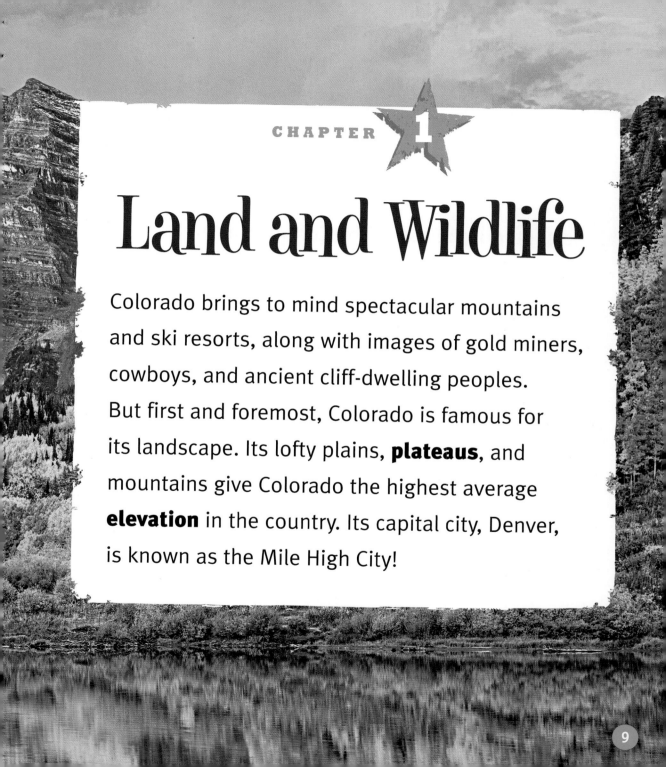

CHAPTER 1

Land and Wildlife

Colorado brings to mind spectacular mountains and ski resorts, along with images of gold miners, cowboys, and ancient cliff-dwelling peoples. But first and foremost, Colorado is famous for its landscape. Its lofty plains, **plateaus**, and mountains give Colorado the highest average **elevation** in the country. Its capital city, Denver, is known as the Mile High City!

An Elevated State

The eastern area of Colorado is part of the Great Plains. These grasslands cover much of the middle United States. The Rocky Mountains cross through the center of the state. The Continental Divide runs along the mountain peaks. It separates streams flowing to the Atlantic Ocean from those flowing to the Pacific Ocean. To the west of the mountains lie gentle rolling hills and the high, flat Colorado Plateau.

There are 53 fourteeners (mountains over 14,000 feet tall) in the State of Colorado.

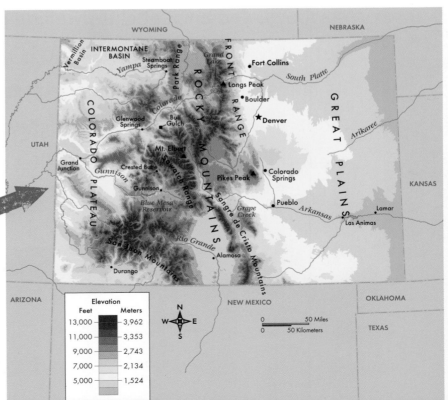

Dinosaur National Monument

For a taste of Colorado's prehistory, visit Dinosaur National Monument. This nationally protected area lies in the northwestern corner of Colorado and crosses into Utah. A range of dinosaur **fossils** can be seen here.

One popular feature is the Wall of Bones (pictured). It displays fossils that are still partially embedded in rock. The monument also includes petroglyphs. These are drawings created by humans thousands of years ago.

Hot springs are a major tourist attraction in places such as Steamboat Springs.

Colorado Waters

A number of rivers snake through the state, including the Colorado River. This famous waterway flows west through the Colorado Plateau. There are also more than 2,000 lakes. Many are scattered through the mountains and fed by melted snow. This makes them cold year-round. For warmer water, check out Colorado's hot springs. These waters are heated by volcanic activity deep underground. They reach the surface at temperatures ranging from pleasantly warm to scalding hot.

What's the Weather?

Colorado is generally quite dry. It receives about 15 inches (38 centimeters) of annual precipitation. However, blizzards do occur across the state during cold winters. Summers stay mild up in the mountains and on the plateau. Lower down, the plains experience temperatures well above 80 degrees Fahrenheit (27 degrees Celsius). The dry heat can lead to forest or grassland fires, which can be started by lightning or human carelessness.

In an average year, Steamboat Springs receives at least some snow more than half of the year.

MAXIMUM TEMPERATURE
114°F

MINIMUM TEMPERATURE
-61°F

The leaves of quaking aspen trees turn a beautiful shade of yellow in fall.

Many Ecosystems

The eastern plains are covered in short grasses with deep root systems. As elevations rise, grasses give way to forests of pine, spruce, and quaking aspen. Higher up are juniper trees and wildflowers such as columbines and lupines. The highest elevations are treeless **tundra**. Here, only short, small flowers and lichen grow. In the west, the plateau is home to desert-loving cactus and sagebrush, as well as pine and aspen trees.

Many animals call Colorado home. Black-tailed prairie dogs are common in the plains. Their tunnel systems are sometimes later claimed by burrowing owls. Black bears, badgers, pocket gophers, and many other mammals live in the mountains. Fish such as trout and chub live in rivers and lakes. Mountain goats and bighorn sheep perch on cliffs, while moose, elk, and deer wander the forests. Swifts, swallows, falcons, and hawks soar through the skies.

Burrowing owls live in tunnels in the ground. Sometimes, they took these tunnels from other burrowing animals, such as prairie dogs or ground squirrels.

The steps of the Colorado state capitol mark where the elevation reaches 1 mile (1.6 km) above sea level.

ONE MILE ABOVE SEA LEVEL

CHAPTER 2

Government

The seat of Colorado's government is its capital city, Denver. This is where the leaders of each of Colorado's branches of government meet and work. Colorado's government is set up much like the U.S. government. It has three branches, each with its own duties and responsibilities. Together, they keep the state safe and strong.

The Three Branches

Led by the governor, Colorado's executive branch enforces the state's laws.

The legislative branch writes laws. It is made up of two houses: the Senate and the House of Representatives. Together, they form the General Assembly.

The judicial branch determines what laws mean and oversees court trials.

COLORADO'S STATE GOVERNMENT

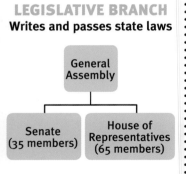

LEGISLATIVE BRANCH
Writes and passes state laws

General Assembly

Senate (35 members)

House of Representatives (65 members)

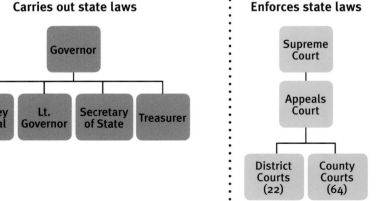

EXECUTIVE BRANCH
Carries out state laws

Governor

Attorney General

Lt. Governor

Secretary of State

Treasurer

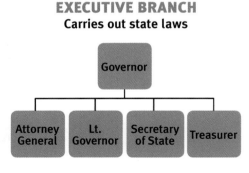

JUDICIAL BRANCH
Enforces state laws

Supreme Court

Appeals Court

District Courts (22)

County Courts (64)

Every voter in Colorado receives a ballot in the mail. Voters can, however, choose to vote in a polling center like this one.

Government by the People

In addition to electing state leaders, the people of Colorado can also play a more direct role in the state's lawmaking process. By gathering enough signatures from their fellow Coloradans, residents can call for a statewide vote to enact new laws, remove officials from office, and more. This gives Colorado's people a strong voice in the way their state is run.

Colorado's National Role

Every state has members in the U.S. Congress. Each state, including Colorado, has two senators. The number of representatives in the House of Representatives depends on a state's population. Colorado has seven.

Each state also has a certain number of votes to apply in the election of the U.S. president. These electoral votes are equal to the number of members of Congress. With two senators and seven representatives, Colorado has nine electoral votes.

2 senators and 7 representatives

9 electoral votes

With nine electoral votes, Colorado's voice in presidential elections is about average compared to other states.

Representing Colorado

Elected officials in Colorado represent a population with a range of interests, lifestyles, and backgrounds.

Ethnicity (2015 estimates)

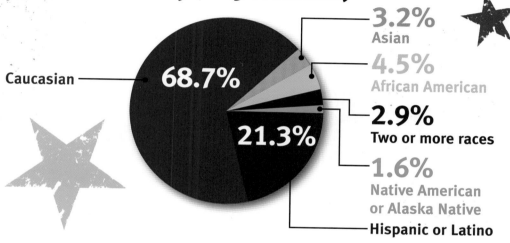

Caucasian — 68.7%

3.2% Asian

4.5% African American

2.9% Two or more races

1.6% Native American or Alaska Native

21.3% — Hispanic or Latino

38% of the population have a degree beyond high school.

64% own their own homes.

86% live in cities.

91% of the population graduated from high school.

10% of Coloradans were born in other countries.

17% speak a language other than English at home.

21

What Represents Colorado?

States choose specific animals, plants, and objects to represent the values and characteristics of the land and its people. Find out why these symbols were chosen to represent Colorado or discover surprising curiosities about them.

Seal

There is a triangle with God's eye at the top of the state seal. The mountains and mining tools below that are symbols of the state's industry and history. At the bottom is the state motto, *nil sine numine*, meaning "nothing without providence" (divine guidance).

Flag

The two blue stripes on Colorado's flag represent the state's sky. The white stripe stands for Colorado's snowcapped mountains. The red C stands for Colorado and its reddish soil.

Claret Cup

STATE CACTUS

This tough and beautiful flowering cactus attracts bees and hummingbirds.

Aquamarine

STATE GEMSTONE

Aquamarine crystals can be found on the peaks of Mount Antero and White Mountain.

Rocky Mountain Columbine

STATE FLOWER

This delicate flower has been Colorado's state flower since 1899 and is strictly protected by law.

Stegosaurus

STATE FOSSIL

A local high school class discovered the Stegosaurus skeleton that is now on display at Denver's Museum of Natural History.

Rocky Mountain Bighorn Sheep

STATE ANIMAL

This type of bighorn sheep is found only in the Rocky Mountains and is known for its balance and agility.

Western Painted Turtle

STATE REPTILE

Two elementary school classes worked together to make the western painted turtle the state reptile.

CHAPTER 3

History

People have lived in Colorado for thousands of years. The area's first residents arrived in about 10,000 BCE. They were hunter-gatherers who stalked animals such as bison, elk, and a species of horse that is now **extinct**. They collected berries, roots, and other valuable plant parts in the forests and prairies. Groups of people moved from place to place, following herds of animals. About 4,000 years ago, however, the lifestyles for some Coloradans changed.

Early Farmers

Beginning in about 2000 BCE, people in Colorado began to farm crops such as corn, beans, and squash. Villages began to develop. In about 100 CE, a new group of farmers settled in

This map shows the general areas where Native American groups settled.

the area: the Ancestral Pueblos. They are named after their villages, which are called pueblos. The Ancestral Pueblos built elaborate buildings out of limestone or clay bricks. In Mesa Verde, an Ancestral Pueblo town was carved into a cliffside! Ancestral Pueblos disappeared in about 1300 CE. No one knows what happened to them.

Later Native Americans

During this time and after, many other groups settled in the region. The Utes were hunter-gatherers who lived mainly in the mountains and desert. These **nomads** had houses that were easy to put up, take down, and carry. The Apaches, Arapahos, and Cheyennes were nomadic groups to the east. These groups followed bison herds, which were a major source of food and other materials.

Ute people built homes called wickiups.

European Interest

In the 1500s, Spanish explorers passed through the area that would become Colorado, but they did not stay. France claimed the land as part of its massive Louisiana Territory in 1682. However, no French settlements were made in Colorado. Sections of the area fell to Spanish hands for a short time. But by 1800, France had regained control. In 1803, it sold the entire Louisiana Territory to the United States.

British Possessions

Louisiana Purchase

Spanish Possessions

N
W   E
S

United States, 1803

Louisiana Purchase

United States Territory, 1803

Present-day state of Colorado

This map shows how the eastern half of Colorado lay within the Louisiana Territory.

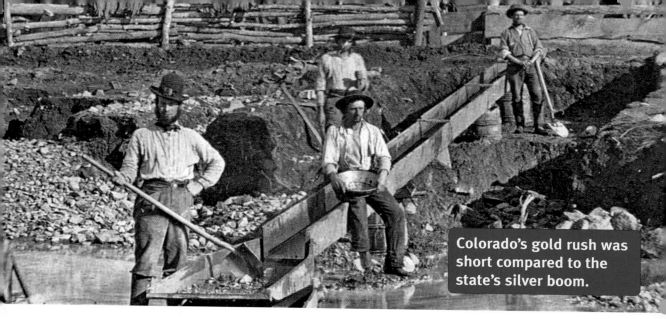

Colorado's gold rush was short compared to the state's silver boom.

Becoming American

European fur trappers wandered the area collecting valuable animal hides during this time. But most residents were Native American. Then, in 1858, gold was found in the mountains. In 1879, silver was also discovered in the area. During the silver boom, miners flooded in, and merchants set up shops to supply them. Ranchers and cowboys moved in, too. The territory's population boomed. In 1876, Colorado was made a state.

More Modern Times

After statehood, Colorado continued to grow. Towns that had started as small mining settlements, such as Denver, became thriving cities. New **irrigation** systems allowed more land than ever to be used for ranching. Mining remained a major part of the state's economy. During World War I (1914–1918), the state was a source of a valuable type of metal called molybdenum.

Timeline of Colorado Events

10,000 BCE
People first settle in what is now Colorado.

1803
France sells the Louisiana Territory to the United States.

10,000 BCE ▶ **100 CE** ▶ **1803** ▶ **1858**

100 CE
Ancestral Pueblos arrive in the area.

1858
Gold is discovered in Colorado.

Colorado played a very different role in World War II (1939–1945). Beginning in 1942, the U.S. government held Japanese Americans in **internment camps**. Japan was fighting the United States in the war, and some people feared anyone of Japanese heritage—even those who lived and worked in this country. As a result, Japanese Americans were forced to leave their homes and move into the camps. Camp Amache, in southeastern Colorado, held more than 7,000 people. After the war, the camp closed.

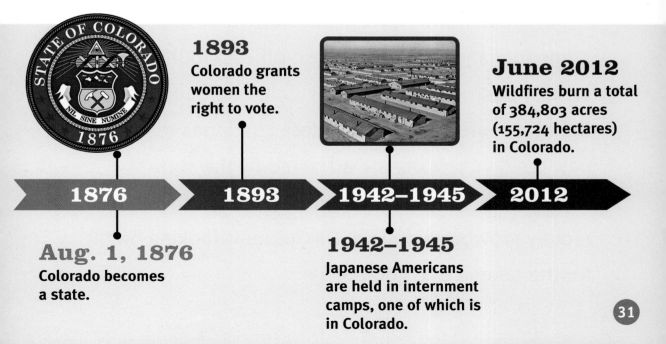

1893
Colorado grants women the right to vote.

June 2012
Wildfires burn a total of 384,803 acres (155,724 hectares) in Colorado.

1876   **1893**   **1942–1945**   **2012**

Aug. 1, 1876
Colorado becomes a state.

1942–1945
Japanese Americans are held in internment camps, one of which is in Colorado.

This early 20th-century trolley in Denver relied on a horse to pull it uphill. When heading downhill, the horse rode the trolley as gravity pulled it along.

In the following decades, Colorado became home to many U.S. government offices. Tourism and other industries grew, helping Colorado boom into the 21st century. Today, the state continues to draw new residents. Many are attracted by the state's incredible beauty. Others come to work in the state's rapidly growing economy. The future is looking bright for the people of Colorado.

Chief Black Kettle and the Sand Creek Massacre

White settlement of Colorado in the 1800s led to conflict with Native Americans. Leaders such as Cheyenne chief Black Kettle worked hard to protect their people. In hopes of peace, some native groups agreed to leave their land and go to **reservations**. Black Kettle moved his people to a small area near Sand Creek in the eastern part of the state. They arrived in September 1864. On November 29, U.S. soldiers attacked the village and killed at least 150 people. The Cheyennes and their Arapaho allies fought back. Some, including Black Kettle, escaped. However, the chief was shot and killed four years later in another battle with U.S. troops.

The Sand Creek Massacre

33

CHAPTER 4

Culture

Colorado's arts reflect the tastes and lives of the people who have called the state home. Native American pottery and weaving are popular. Artists also make jewelry of silver, turquoise, and blue lapis lazuli. The state's history and landscape have shaped several authors' works, from Louis L'Amour's classic westerns to Diane Mott Davidson's modern mysteries. The mountains, plains, and plateaus also fill many canvases, as some of Colorado's most well-known painters are famed for their landscapes.

Sports in the Mountains

Sports fans in Colorado can watch the Denver Broncos play football or the Colorado Rockies play baseball. The Denver Nuggets represent the state in the National Basketball Association (NBA). Hockey fans cheer for the Colorado Avalanche. Colorado also offers a lot of opportunities for residents to take part in the action themselves. Skiing, snowboarding, hiking, and mountain climbing are all popular mountain sports. The towns of Aspen and Vail are home to world famous ski resorts.

Colorado has just the right climate for skiers, with a lot of snow and plenty of sunshine.

A musician performs at the Colorado Cowboy Poetry Gathering.

Colorado Celebrations

In Colorado, you're never far from a piece of fascinating history or a view of towering mountains. This has given the state's culture much of its flavor and texture. Visitors can look at art and listen to traditional mariachi bands. Or they can sit and enjoy the annual Colorado Cowboy Poetry Gathering in Golden. You'll soon learn to expect the unexpected when it comes to Colorado culture.

At Work

Mining is still a major part of Colorado's economy. Gold, silver, copper, molybdenum, and titanium are some of the state's biggest mining products. Ranches and farms also remain important. Most ranchers raise cattle. Others raise sheep, pigs, and other livestock. Some Coloradans work in manufacturing, often making electronics or airplane parts. The state's biggest employer is the service industry. This includes hotels, restaurants, and many jobs associated with tourism.

Sheep in Colorado may be raised for wool or meat.

Changes in the Mines

Colorado mining has evolved over the years as people's needs changed. In World War I, the United States had a desperate need for molybdenum, so more molybdenum mines opened in Colorado. The focus switched to oil and coal in the late 20th century, when the nation had trouble getting enough of these resources from other countries. However, minerals are limited. Colorado mining can't last forever. With this in mind, the state has brought in other industries to create more jobs.

What's for Dinner?

With cattle ranches thriving across Colorado, it's no surprise that beef is a popular food. Dishes range from steaks to stews. Chili is another common meal. This hearty soup uses beans and tomatoes as a base. Some chili recipes stick to vegetables. Others include ground beef. Extra spice is supplied by chili peppers, which give the soup its name.

 Denver Omelet

Ask an adult to help you!

This omelet is named for Colorado's capital city. No one knows exactly why this dish got its name, but it is a tasty meal.

Ingredients
Butter-flavored cooking spray
1/2 cup diced ham
1/2 cup chopped onions
1/2 cup chopped red or
   green bell peppers

3 eggs
2 tablespoons water
1/2 tablespoon butter

Directions
Coat a frying pan lightly with cooking spray. Heat to medium high. Add the ham, onions, and bell peppers and cook until browned. Turn off the heat and set the pan aside. In a small bowl, whisk together the eggs and water. Melt the butter in an omelet pan set to medium high. Pour in the eggs. Wait about 30 seconds, then lower the heat to medium low. Allow the eggs to set (about 3 to 5 minutes). Remove the pan from the heat. Top the eggs with the ham mixture. Use a spatula to fold the edges of the omelet over the filling.

Beautiful Colorado

It is obvious there is a lot to see and do in Colorado. Residents and visitors alike can explore the state's beautiful landscape, rich history, and vibrant culture. How about a brisk walk in the Rockies or a hot bowl of chili? A visit to a historical site? What will you want to do? ★

Hikers enjoy the view near Silverton.

Famous People

James Beckwourth

(ca. 1798–1867) was a fur trapper and explorer who blazed a trail westward across the United States. He eventually settled in Denver.

Kit Carson

(1809–1868) was an explorer, trapper, and guide who befriended several Native American groups. During the Civil War, he helped defend Colorado from Confederate forces.

Ouray

(1833–1880) was a Ute chief in western Colorado. He worked to make peace between his people and the white settlers who came to the area in the 1800s.

Nikola Tesla

(1856–1943) was a scientist and inventor who made many contributions to our knowledge of electricity. He conducted many of his experiments in Colorado Springs.

The Unsinkable Molly Brown

(1867–1932) was a wealthy passenger aboard the *Titanic* who famously ordered people aboard a lifeboat to return to the sinking ship in search of survivors. Her real name was Margaret "Molly" Brown, and she lived in Denver.

John Denver

(1943–1997) was a singer-songwriter and actor who liked Colorado so much that he named himself after the city of Denver. He wrote many songs about his favorite state, including "Rocky Mountain High," one of Colorado's official state songs.

Don Cheadle

(1964–) is an Academy Award–nominated actor who has appeared in films such as *Ocean's Eleven* and the *Iron Man* and *Avengers* series. He went to high school in Denver.

Amy Adams

(1974–) is the Academy Award–nominated star of such films as *Arrival*, *The Muppets*, and *Enchanted*. She grew up in Castle Rock.

Chauncey Billups

(1976–) is a five-time NBA All-Star who played professional basketball for 17 seasons. He was born and raised in Denver.

Missy Franklin

(1995–) is a swimmer and five-time Olympic gold medalist who set a world record for the 200-meter backstroke in 2012. She grew up in Centennial.

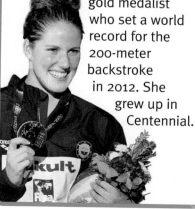

Did You Know That ...

Colorado's highest point is the peak of Mount Elbert, at 14,440 feet (4,401 meters). Its lowest point is the Arikaree River, at 3,315 feet (1,010 m).

Colorado has 8,000 miles (12,875 kilometers) of rivers and more than 2,000 lakes.

Some of the ancient bristlecone pine trees that grow in Colorado are more than 2,000 years old.

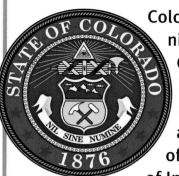

Colorado got its nickname, the Centennial State, because it became a state 100 years after the signing of the Declaration of Independence.

Each year 500,000 people ascend Pikes Peak.

Colorado is home to four national parks: Mesa Verde National Park, Rocky Mountain National Park, Great Sand Dunes National Park and Preserve, and Black Canyon of the Gunnison National Park.

Did you find the truth?

 T People have farmed in Colorado since about 2000 BCE.

F Colorado was one of the 13 original U.S. states.

Resources

Books

Nonfiction

Somervill, Barbara A. *Colorado*. New York: Children's Press, 2014.

Zeiger, Jennifer. *Rocky Mountain National Park*. New York: Children's Press, 2018.

Fiction

Avi. *Hard Gold: The Colorado Gold Rush of 1859: A Tale of the Old West*. New York: Hyperion Books for Children, 2008.

Hobbs, Will. *Bearstone*. Carmel, CA: Hampton-Brown, 2004.

Naylor, Phyllis Reynolds. *The Fear Place*. New York: Atheneum Books for Young Readers, 1994.

Movies

American Flyers (1985)

City Slickers (1991)

The Dog Who Saved Christmas Vacation (2010)

Downhill Racer (1969)

Harvey (1950)

Ice Castles (1978)

The Unsinkable Molly Brown (1964)

Visit this Scholastic website for more information on Colorado:
★ www.factsfornow.scholastic.com
Enter the keyword **Colorado**

Important Words

elevation (el-uh-VAY-shuhn) height above sea level

extinct (ik-STINGKT) no longer found alive

fossils (FAH-suhlz) bones, shells, or other traces of an animal or plant from millions of years ago, preserved as rock

internment camps (in-TURN-muhnt KAMPS) confined areas where Japanese Americans were forced to live during World War II

irrigation (ir-uh-GAY-shuhn) the process of supplying water to crops by artificial means

nomads (NOH-madz) people who move from place to place without permanent homes

plateaus (pla-TOHZ) areas of level ground that are higher than the surrounding area

reservations (rez-ur-VAY-shuhnz) areas of land set aside by the government for a special purpose

tundra (TUHN-druh) a very cold area where there are no trees and the soil under the surface of the ground is always frozen

Index

Page numbers in **bold** indicate illustrations.

About the Author

Jennifer Zeiger's favorite memories are of the time she spent as a kid at Crow Canyon Archaeological Center and the surrounding region. Today, she lives in Chicago, Illinois, where she writes and edits books for children.